# VIXEN

# VIXEN

*Glenda Beagan*

*with woodcuts by Jenny Fell*

HONNO *POETRY*

Published by Honno
'Ailsa Craig', Heol y Cawl, Dinas Powys
Wales CF6 4AH

First Impression 1996

**British Library Cataloguing in Publication Data**

A catalogue record for this book is available from the British Library

ISBN 1 870206 20 7

*Published with the financial support of
the Arts Council of Wales*

Cover illustration by Jenny Fell
Cover design by Emma Cox and Emma Veitch

Typeset and printed in Wales by Dinefwr Press, Llandybïe

*I fy mam, Trixie,*
*ac er cof am fy nhad,*
*Clydwyn*

# ACKNOWLEDGEMENTS

Some of these poems have previously appeared in:

> *The Anglo-Welsh Review, Borderlines, Connections, Dragon, Encounter, The New Welsh Review, Outposts, Planet, Poetry Review, Poetry Wales, Resurgence, Tears in the Fence, Wood and Water.*

Others have been prize-winners or runners-up in the Aberystwyth Open Poetry Competitions.

# CONTENTS

WINGBEATS

Wingbeats                                          3
Soothsayer                                         4
Cofio Rhydgaled                                    6
Gaia                                               7
Blodeuwedd                                         9
Arianrhod                                         10
Epona                                             11
Rhiannon                                          13
Moel Maenefa                                      14
Boudicca                                          16
Morrigan                                          17
Melangell                                         18


VIXEN RUN

Vixen Totem                                       23
Vixen                                             26
Landship                                          27
A Tree: Its Purpose                               29
In Vixen Country                                  30
From Quarry Cottage                               32
Three Thoughts on the Artifice of Gardens         33
The Exultation of the Vixen                       35
Fox-mother                                        36


THE WISDOM OF THE PLACE

Handfast                                          41
Novella                                           43
A Glimpse from the Shed                           44
Cats by the Sea                                   45

Y Goderau                        46
The Secret                       47
The Captain                      48
In the Rigging                   49
The Window Cleaner               50
Ultrasound Scan                  51
Replay                           53
Roulette                         54
Heirlooms                        55
Discoveries                      56
The Collector                    57
Kalends                          58
Lure                             59
Ceremonial                       60
Victrix                          61
Manikin                          62
Bryn Mair                        64
Triskel                          66
Shaman                           67
The Wisdom of the Place          69

# WINGBEATS

*Wingbeats*
*Soothsayer*
*Cofio Rhydgaled*
*Gaia*
*Blodeuwedd*
*Arianrhod*
*Epona*
*Rhiannon*
*Moel Maenefa*
*Boudicca*
*Morrigan*
*Melangell*

# Wingbeats

Sometimes
she would find in the dry bleach
of her yard, walnut shells,
furrowed husks only. Birds must have dropped
them from high up in the paleness
and tall wheezing dust of summer, pollen
and crisped earth.

Before
she could only love thin, ice-minded men
of caution and bone. It was high and airless
in that country. Febrile, she was forever
mountain gulping, cut, bruised on scree slopes
where birds were dull metals, eagles
with cold eyes. Even summer on those bare scarps
was only a tanning wind, a hint of small thorn flowers.

She would set the walnut shells
(so much the small round boats of Celtic saints
who took to the tides and the sea's heaving,
pilgrims of chance and gulls' voices)
on her wide sill, with her lemon geraniums,
the scent of them, sunlight amplified on glass,
strata of compacted flowerings.

This is different.
There is nothing thin or ice-minded
about this man. She is watching him like a cat,
afraid of her own fierceness. From her kitchen
she can see his boots on the scaffolding. Their dustiness
scuffles her heart. She hears him above her. He is
partridges in the feathery grass. He is peppers
and melons and the juice of redcurrants.
Each movement he makes is a song for her.

He lives in his body
like wine in a glass
she tilts and savours.

And a walnut tree grew in the dry bleach of her yard.

## Soothsayer

it is this taking
this gripping
of the word
that is new to us

we were taught
to slide with the word
to smooth things
to make the surface
pleasing

to use words like this
is tearing us
it uproots us from ourselves
we must split the flesh
to get at the peachstone

but it hurts, it hurts
we are not accustomed

I was afraid
I was using language
I had never used it before

watch your language
they said
she uses language
they said
a portcullis came down on their eyes

I was on the outside

before
there was a secret speech
I did not say

I could make my marks
on a hidden paper
I could write it down
I could tear it up

it was not for their eyes
it was the truth

now it is out in the open
I have begun
now
I must see if I can stand it

## Cofio Rhydgaled

I am running again
running against arrows

I am not on your side

I am in the ditch again
hiding
hearing the horses

I am not on your side

under the lip of the rock again
waiting
with my blade
the one my brother made

so you're looking for me again
are you
whoever you are

you won't find me
you don't even know me
I may address you civilly
if I have to

but I'm watching you all the time

if I'm running against arrows
I am not on your side

# Gaia

You have been here before
you know the moment when the sea stops
the tides suspend themselves
coiled in your hand
you taste the bud before it forms
trace growth of an elaborate mycelium
in the black air dot spore

you have been here before
you know where the harrier hangs
in wimpled heights
you hold the reins of more than horses
histories emerge from eyes
heavens from nostrils
you fold and gather floods and carcases
stock your fisheries with nameless forces
let them trickle through the sluice of your whims
if it pleases you

sometimes it pleases you to do nothing at all
but sit all day on a bare hill
to soothe the wildeyed winter daughters
the mottled ewes
you have been here before
you knew Ffordd Ffrainc when the chain mail warriors
bristled through beechwoods
turned mothers and babies from their doors
and fired their damp and putrid cottages
with that same mechanical dutiful sadness
soldiers wear about their butchery

you knew the wild boar and the bear
you suckled the orphaned wolf cubs
made a home for yourself among damson trees
spent whole seasons lacing tributaries
with lichen and elderflower
tending, waiting, patient for so long
till crops and flocks sprang from your fingers
all among fens and salt flats
laughed when you made the eastern wind your lover
and bared your legs to the snow

I see you sometimes
sat quite still
hid in the grey orchard

knowing you the way I do
I keep out of your way, mostly
remembering

## Blodeuwedd

Lust was the loom
I was woven on
the man who webbed me
knowing nothing
human. Frost
were the eyes
that pulled me
into life for Lleu,
but when he was gone
I was lonely for Gronw
and how was that wrong?

I am glad to be free
to flit among
dank trees. Smells
are meanings for me;
scuttlings speak.
Out of coppiced hazels I skim
into blue light, the moon fingering
me. My feathers are glad to be
dipped in wind. After my catchings
I sit on a bough and clean myself.
So how is this punishment?

# Arianhod

Out of dulse
and sea-girdle
you wove a ship
of the mind
to trick me:

cordwain of gold,
kingfisher's colours,
leather vanities
for my feet's softness,
until illusion

trapped me, a whole
false fleet about
my rock's crown. Math,
unmatched magus,
why was it Gwydion

you taught, when it was I,
Don's daughter, who lived ripe
for such lore? I would not
have seen the cantrefs ravaged,
your foot-maiden shamed.

Yet from the sea's cradle
my sons swept, secrets torn
into life by Math's wand, one a wave
in brightness, one not to be named to suffer,
bleeding in wizardry's tree.

You, Gwydion, who stole fleetness
of deer, dark heart of boar and wolf's hunger to augment
your guile, take this from me, your sister –
for the men you have seen butchered for a whim,
for those lost blossoms you wove for sorrow,

hate, pure and heartless as the wind.

*Epona*

I had seen your carvings
crude
      stylized
            potent

you were sat side-saddle
facing us
wearing a pleated robe

your pony was jaunty
your nose was Roman
your hair was pushed into curls

your mouth
was a mouth a child might scrape in clay;
firm and straight
with a stick

you were not in the least delicate
you had large hands and feet

you were the sort to roll up your sleeves
and start working

*there is a white horse cut in the chalk scarp*

I could, perhaps, have seen you there
riding, riding

a twist of gold in your hair

a sudden thaw had turned the world to mirrors
your levels were bright metals
and I was here

not looking for you
not even thinking of you

scanning the valley, its glittering planes
its birds, its glare, its beads of white,
its light, its wings beating

you were bringing the horses
not leading the horses
simply bringing the horses
as clouds bring rain

laughing, your hair wild
running, not riding
a herd at your shoulder
no more than a child

# Rhiannon

find me
under the owl window
I smile
I am not what I seem
sat, clad simply,
carding wool

old woman at the edge of life
now, with time's loosening
how should it be other than this:
these palsied hands,
these shadows?

drowsy, I see
small smoke of bees
lift from the keps
at the orchard edge

pulse of the land
its coiled gold
its glimmering combs
its sweetness

bring me no bishop and his book
bring me no kindly simperings
cold piety would kill my worlds
of falcons, hounds
and steeds white as anemones

I let them think I have lost my wits
this way I keep my flickerings
the dappled harvest in my lap
the charmed birds on my sill

I am my past
not this dull shape
I am my loves
my laughing hair

bodies of heroes burn in me
wasps sing in ripe red air

## Moel Maenefa

Hafod
of the clawed
heart

shelter
of the stormed
people

below this scarp of horsemen,
this battle table
Tremeirchion blinks

in the sun, scanning the valley's width
to the sea, Dinorben's
eaten mountain

Maenefa,
solitary stone
in your cropped

ring, focus
of sheeptrails, vortex
of ancient trackways

below their windbreak
ewes lift quiet faces,
chomp incuriously

where Offa's earthen
ramparts bulge
I watch the new road

burgeon, its smooth curve
cambering that Roman straightness
of Rhuallt hill

on the bridle path
a tumult of finches cries
in dried keys

after long drought
the rains have blessed
a crop of livid cups

saffron buttons,
puffballs, stinkhorns
mushrooms of rich meat

before this fresh October green
the earth was Mexican; dust
capered in coughing winds

here above the dozers' hum
the dumpers' whirr,
the sound of clanged

and bullied metal, these
cleansing skies
unclench and pacify

over St Beuno's
the tall cross
lurches in bracken

while barbed wire, sharpening
with light, aches
to the triangulation point

greygolds of flint shards
glint among sheepdirt's
globes of bright jet

## Boudicca

I can be free
under the sky, washed
in bright air. I can
fly, canny falcon, over flanks
of long hills, shoulders
of windflexed barley.

Here, oak and lichen
mix with willow carr.
Streams of sharp cresses
course in this land as blood
hums in my body. This is earth
I know and love as they never can.

A people of clarity,
their straight lines, their searing light
have shunned the smell of beast and byre.
Dung and mulch, the breath of horses, are part
of me, as much as the twittering of martins
in the thatch, the seep of spring water.

Their palaces of tile and brick
would thin our strength. Near them
I hunger soon to clothe myself in woodsmoke,
feel again warm loam under my feet,
drink the strength of mare's milk.
For some, not least the man I must call husband,

their softness calls,
but I have seen their flagons of glass
the colour of damsons, sipped tangy wine,
whitebubbled, stared them out,
returning to rough mead, the withy cart's
wild speed, the tearing blade.

## Morrigan

War-bird,
sometimes I tire of battle,
screams of the dying
stench of carrion
smoke from burnt thatch.

Raven, friend,
you draw your sustenance
from plucked dead eyes. I seek
an essence, the distillation
of man's enmity.

In times of peace
I shrink inside myself, grow
small and faint. Folk might see
merely a woman walking, dark birds wheeling.
I am emptied of power.

Now it is well past Lammas,
a season of long warm rains.
Kine stand idly, bangled in vapour.
Crops rot in drenched fields.
Soon will come raids, revenges.

At Samhain
I come into my strength,
feeding on shadows. Oracle
and curse together, I am heard
as a howl on an edge of snow.

Warriors know
I must live out my doom as they do,
that lavishing in death I touch the sky.
So who is to know of the questions I tear
like sinews, the lack at the core?

Your feathers flick thinly, raven, rusty in wind.

## Melangell

They call me saint.
They bless me and the hares they call my lambs,
here, in quietness of forest, fastness
of mountain wall.

Pennant is my place,
mellow paps the hills behind my home,
dappled cones sunlight plays upon,
with clouds dancing.

Fierce beasts were the waves
that tossed me, my landfall so
far west of here. Through winter's mire and frost
I struggled.

A carlin, hooped
in age gave me bowed wisdom, broth
in a dish of bone, simples and salves.
The body mends at last.

The spirit grows
to a glade's calm, chill of well water,
bannocks of coarse flour. I delve and hew,
Erin remembering:

Tanat rejoicing.
Then comes the summer of mallows and wild lupins
blue as streams on soft banks of seed,
the cry of the hunt,

the blare and wild
will of hounds, till through birches they come like a fire
running, a hare at my hem, a huntsman's horn singed
to his lips in a blister of sound.

They call it miracle,
and so it was, I, frozen in his prince's sight, never
having seen a man so like a god, a flame. His name is Brochwel
and I, a bride of Christ . . .

My hares, my lambs
are sweet velvet nutmegs. I have seen them dancing
in moonlight. At the *prie dieu* I leave posies
of white broom.

Maidens flock here,
craving this rule, this life I blend. As years
mount the arch of the sky, I kneel and whisper,
plaiting staunch cords of peace.

# VIXEN RUN

*Vixen Totem*

*Vixen*

*Landship*

*A Tree: Its Purpose*

*In Vixen Country*

*From Quarry Cottage*

*Three Thoughts on the Artifice of Gardens*

*The Exultation of the Vixen*

*Fox-mother*

## Vixen Totem

### i

St Dyfnog's well
means spindly young holly trees
moist red clay
hart's tongue ferns
crimped by long frost
snowdrops sprinkled
among the ivy
around the well
where vixen steps
gingerly

she is like a cat today

vixen,
you are more mysterious
than a dog could ever be

dogs are too human

you have the singularity of the cat
who lives with humans
but remains her own cat

I would be like that

### ii

never be
sentimental about vixen
she is, after all, a killer

this is her territory

it is my privilege
to sit with her above the world

vixen places her head on her paws
she breathes wheezily
she is not young anymore

so quiet among the clouds

within the waves
of wind and light
you can hear the blackthorn
crackle

white ponies watch us
toss their manes

with the pylons humming
with the transmitter
crowning the summit of the hill behind us

through sparkles of silverweed
in sparse grass
through stars of milk quartz

it's the wind that makes us

that anarchic something in thin air


iii

at Tyddyn Benlli
she finds rich pickings

red ochre earth
red clover
a venerable seaside donkey now retired
slant light
swivels on a chimney cowl
and polishes the greenhouse
and the old porcelain bathtub
where the gander stands guard with his wives

among carline thistles
and flying ants
it's not that comfortable
what's more, hencoops and sutured sheds
are not that picturesque

24

but from this distance
this high up
the land below shows all its indentations
saucers and cups
in the Celtic fields
umber and amber

the goose quill at my feet


                              iv

it's an autumn of blackberry silver
I'm walking with vixen under the moon
skirting the edge of the quarry

night cries
shrew sirens
a dog barks

under the hazels
the low shapes of house
huddle in starwash, the ricks, the grey barns

about us
            the owl
                        makes her own white orbit
                                        of silences

## Vixen

motherhood peels me bare
like a willow wand
some small child scrapes in the road
or throws in the pond

motherhood aches me pale
I bleed with my child's wound
and hurt with his friend's unfriendliness
I climb with his bruise

motherhood grows me brave
now no mere woman nor wife
the vixen who fights for her cubs
will fight for her life

## Landship

It's like a lantern,
the conservatory
frosted
multifaceted

now, in this heavily moving
night of cloud and moonwind
we seem to be sailing

but we are deeply rooted
here, in The Vineyard
the deep freeze whirrs into action
on the other side of the house
the telephone is ringing softly
inconsequentially
and someone answers it

I am standing alone
listening to the humming of the house
in the diastole of starlight
outside, a broad oak
centuries old
stands guard beside its whispering sisters

they are young
and a little fickle
they are the plumes of the pampas grass

I inhabit the air
heady, vine scented
cold with the sharpness of night
and night's undeciphered noises
invisible
in fields around
are fine black-faced Suffolks
warm Friesians of sound mind

beyond the yellow vineleaves
(their tendrils on the glass
make a filigree chiaroscouro)
I know there is stout fencing
a long asphalt drive
and a white iron gate
that needs oiling

I know the owl is my friend
that the moon is my familiar
that the foxes and pheasants
in the coverts and copses abounding
are all of my keeping

as I go sailing

## A Tree: Its Purpose

the tank where cattle drink
is oozy green at the corners
its surface is bespattered with blue flies
and where the pipe joins, it rusts a little

water falling loose on stone
helps make a muddier circle
near the gate where beasts of patience
wait for the milking

I like their smell
it reminds me of something good
I like their eyes
their hazing breath

to stand so still so long
and see continuum of fields
pale parsonage and post bus in the lane
and never know what a tree is

not the word

only its texturedness
its rough utility
scraping the rise of your back where the itch is

# In Vixen Country

to walk in the glistening land
among the bubbled water
and the scratched stones

to move down the sheep slopes
from wet bilberry green
and willow herb
through browned summer foxgloves

to the shrivelled old alders
by the dried lake's margin
and wonder how
when all things look the same
the shining has left them

the shining in the heart

the donkey brays
the Guinea fowl
the dark exotic one
moves among the bantams

like a dowager

her plumes
her plump sequinned flanks
frame on shaped elegance

all the old pungencies are there
elder dust
mingled with sun and dung
ragwort and yarrow

goslingdown
thistledown
float through sharp air
to the ramshackle clattering huts

the wind lifts unceremoniously

battening down
the hatches of a mind
that outgrew the glistening

and peeled itself thin

## From Quarry Cottage

a concrete tank, stained
a metal ladder hanging
and a gauge and a wheeltap
and then rough ground
where the goats pull taut
on their ropes and lick globe flowers
in the cloudy undecided morning
whether it will rain

Joan bakes in paper cases
feeds the range with blanched splits
turns out the small green jellies
now they are set
lays them on trays out ready in the back

the geese make sudden crash
(it says BEWARE OF THE GEESE on the gate)
seeing the man's outline on the quarry

they keep breaking down the fencing,
the boys from the village, as soon as it's mended
and yet says the man from head office
imagine the outcry if a kid fell
there'd be no end of it

the man has a gun and a dog
is looking for rabbits
sees all the blackberries
but it's too early for them yet

the geese have stopped
are still
Joan dries her hands

it's time to pick her grandson up from school

*Three Thoughts on the Artifice of Gardens*

i

bits of wet straw
and sycamore
freak through the windy garden
and settle
at the feet
of the Chinese lantern tree

the hexagonal summer house
is painted white
it looks like a cake
its tiny winecoloured window panes
were once
the very latest thing

a white cat
sits in the laurels
unaware
that gazebos
and delicately scented Oriental foliage
are not, after all
everything

ii

twin terracotta owls
guard the gateway
this half light
among the sumacs
and the coppery skyline
was meant for them

startled
by their own sculpted exuberance
they're poised
for ceramic flight,
custodians
of opulent memory

and then the night begins

iii

the moon is full of frost
swimming freestyle
over the conservatory

the yellow vine leaves
shuffle to the floor
lie there
the gilded amputated hands
of goddesses

each time
metallic whispers
as they kiss the tiles

the grapes are very small
and sharp
and sweet

somewhere a vixen
punctuates the hush
with her own
rather more fundamental
rhapsody

## The Exultation of the Vixen

I lie in the night of the world
I think of the creatures
of the colours of the creatures
of their strangeness

I am one with them there
with each sleek beast
with the soft scrabbling vole in her home
in the root of the great elder

now fanned with lace
now flamed with summer moths

I am one with them there
moving imperceptibly
I'm sallow white and furred
I'm the tiny ghost of a snowy owl
in the warm core of the darkness

I lie in the night of the world
I think of the creatures
of the colours of the creatures
of their strangeness

then comes that fear again
that vicarious frosted moment
the exultation of the vixen sloping in her grove
and calling her fierce sadness

## Fox-mother

I am fox-mother.
Encountering me
at the edge of the spinney,
marauder in ferns,

finds me lithe
in the fox-light.
I am half seen only.
An edge of crispness

in the trees
merges with lace of cold branches,
mist breath of the fields.
I am a dance at the core of your eye.

Ghost am I,
scourge of plump quail,
spirit of quill and feather?
Bantams in the peeled coop

squeal in their sleep. They dream of me
as death angel, quick ginger queen,
plucking them clean. I am
their musky destiny: white tooth,

purposed claw. My cubs flex
in bracken, off the lane
to Aberkinsey in a cliff of sand,
I teach patience and stealth,

moonlesson walking; how with ease
to slip, lissom as water
over the lip of a weir, to blend
with kale and corn, to seem

a mirage among larches. I blur
identities in briars and pines,
hugging remnants of orchards.
I am sharpness you saw in shadow.

I am fox-mother –
hard-bitten guardian
of the sly ditch; red bitch,
swift thief, svelte killer.

# THE WISDOM OF THE PLACE

*Handfast*
*Novella*
*A Glimpse from the Shed*
*Cats by the Sea*
*Y Goderau*
*The Secret*
*The Captain*
*In the Rigging*
*The Window Cleaner*
*Ultrasound Scan*
*Replay*
*Roulette*
*Heirlooms*
*Discoveries*
*The Collector*
*Kalends*
*Lure*
*Ceremonial*
*Victrix*
*Manikin*
*Bryn Mair*
*Triskel*
*Shaman*
*The Wisdom of the Place*

# Handfast

This place has its siren voice.
You'll find that you cannot leave it.
Pagodas of viper's bugloss in wet grass,
raindropped umbellifers, thronging
the green tunnel where the quarry railway ran,
all grow numinous, all hold you,
speak of a life you lived before,
familiar, here in the old meadow
scented with may, with hay of lost seasons.

You are one of their fetchings.
You won't go.
Your nervous scudding birds grown in deep
   leaves
shimmer the pond on take off.
They don't get far.
They circle the pines up on Flagstaff Hill.
They skim the willow carr and the tangled alders,
returning, as if a magnet drew them,
back to this place, specific, theirs.

And yours. You'll get that you don't want to leave.
The idea becomes absurd. You'll laugh at the
   thought of it.
Here you have everything. All you need.
There are goats in the sunny churchyard,
shaped serenity, buff-coloured ruminants
among the stones. I could watch them for hours.
They look so wise. There are hens in the dappled
   orchard,
such a comforting sound, like a chuckling.

Yes, we breathe an air of enchantment.
Accept it. Respond to it.
Is it real? But of course it is.
Julian's repairing the windmill.
Kay bakes all the bread.
How real do you want things to be?

I shall sit here for a while. It's so warm.
Have you noticed how the midges
cling to that one spot,
hovering over that dip at the end?
They're like a black cloud.
It's so peaceful.
Even the birds seem too sleepy to sing.
Just listen.
Hush.
Give me your hand.

# Novella

Beyond the pond, the stabling block, the cupola
and here under the archway where the carriages would
    turn
and young grooms held the horses' heads, beyond all
    these,
the ha-ha and the lawns, the folly, that Gothic toy
the joke of some inventive defunct lord,
beyond the dances on the polished floors
and all the formal fictive patternings,
there is a kind of seepage from the past,
a gesture or a practised mannerism
plumed like a courtier's euphonious nonsense.

You wonder where the pattern went,
the scullions and the still room maids.
A squinting girl bears a jug of hot water for her
    ladyship,
is not admitted to her room, you understand,
being undecorative . . . the exuberance of the hounds,
fine-mettled creatures, the candelabra and the family
    plate
with, out of sight, the tinklings of a harpsichord,
topiary pheasants, the girl at the lodge gate,
a furtive glance, a half smile from the heir,
a sudden irridescence in his eyes
records the copper in her hair.

Someone moves in an old orchard in September air.
The simplest understated wind will warm and turn
those grasses, bleached of colour, dried into speech
decoding the patina of an antique summer's heat.
A collie there, white-muzzled, lifts its head
observes with its milky eye then settles into sleep
against the wall. She picks some Victoria plums
and holds the boughs, then lets the wind catch them,
lets the wind shake them, lets the wind take
whatever memories there are in this other outer place
beyond the pond, beyond the crumbling cupola.

# A Glimpse from the Shed

I liked the shed, how, even in winter
when all things were sodden and dark,
it spoke of summer, its scents, its sureness.
Something to do with crocus corms,
dahlia tubers wrapped in browning newspaper
as if a lick of flame had singed it, twine,
rolled chicken wire, stacked shallow trays for
     seedlings,
tools in a row, the secateurs, the oil can on the ledge.

I am reminded of all the gardens.

Here, walled and secretive
I played all one bluegold day
finding overgrown paths,
gazebos smelling of creosote.

Here, where you loved to drowse,
nodding on phlox and lavender
was a place where I knew love came steady,
dependable as tap water.

I keep seeing the shed,
the one broken pane,
that piece of perspex replacement
forced loose after equinox gales.

I can still see the swing in the door,
hear the squeak of the chain,
tied by the scent of earth in a fine sieve,
strands of robin's nest in a drainpipe.

Now all these glimpses point to one place,
to one enclosed wonder
where men and women sit in classic ease,
their children ample as strawberries.

*Cats by the Sea*

This is the season between.
The sun is white.
Sea and sky are slashed brush strokes:
petrol, ultramarine. A black boat
sits in pink pebbles, slid on an edge.
Speckled green, speckled white,
like the scribblings on birds' eggs,
the sloped bank shifts
with a grey cat's slink.

Her paws make soft cautious shapes.
Her eyes watch the wind quest among weeds.

Behind that row of fishermen's cottages,
whitewashed or weatherboarded,
pantiled or roofed with tar,
the poor cats, the wild homeless ones,
come running in to the shadow harbour,
swift tails in sharp angled light on the quay.

In the lee of the old Customs House,
its high lofts, its tariff sheet proud on the wall
in quaint eighteenth-century copperplate,
the S's looped like hieroglyphs,
they pluck the air in their hunger,
the salt fishy air. They follow the slime,
the rainbow scales to the dock, where men in deep
    thigh boots
drag crates of herring and gulls slice shining.

Foregrounded, sat on a cushion on a wide sill,
is a different being, a duchess among cats.
She is framed by white, white of the casement,
white of the fringed curtains. She has placed herself
to perfection on violet lozenges of watered silk.

# Y Goderau

Stone fishtraps that the brothers built
measure the shore with standing trays of water,
a finer grey on grey. The pebbles are complete,
set by a grouping ordering intelligence
in graded rows of shade and size and shape
as if they were all massed eggs of some rock bird,
carved out of rock and lifting its rock wings
embossed with a clamorous seal.

It is a world of grey, a world like a Zen garden
that knows and holds the discipline of peace.
Cistercians shaped these hollows for their use,
for the scaled and quivering harvest of the sea
and the tides still cling through the centuries
to the tanks they made. Though they're shallower
their rectangular coolness and their liquid squares
frame these mackerel skies the same. They celebrate
their formal patterns calmly. They are plain things.

## The Secret

You do not know my country,
how, invisibly, whinnying horses
wake us at first light
from drenched fields,
how geese scold in scabby paddocks
where orchards thin, and so many things
have been abandoned,

simply
to lie in bleached grass
gathering light and rainwater:
porcelain bathtubs, old lobster pots
painted a harsh yellow
and weighted with rocks.
You do not know my country,

why the men have grown taciturn
(it was not always so), why
the women's proud discipline
is still their stillness.
It is in the landscape though, this sheen
of waiting, just as lisps and rustles
shape the speech of the high beech hedges.

As a child
I thought these trees grew tall
to touch God's table, that behind them
were palaces with kings of lace.
But no, they are only windbreaks
guarding long fields of beet and kale,
harsh grids of sluices and white churches.

Do not ask
what happened in my country.
From the lanes you can still climb
to the empty places,
circles, avenues of thorn,
cold houses whee they keep behind tall glass
marks of the old language carved on soft stone.

## The Captain

Through the tiered streets of the fishermen's cottages
and up to the grander villas in the sun,
some with cream painted porticoes and porches,
their plots all marked with scallop shells and patterns
of red pebbles, you'll climb and find a house
that stands alone to face the sea. A layered garden
dips to the cliff's brink where a cracked seat perches.
The subsidence makes sitting out unsafe
but looks on rocks where oystercatchers range in warmth
and splashing spray, and all the air is summery with bees
among the leggy lavender and unstaked pinks.
He likes to potter there, pretending to read the paper,
taking his tea outside on an old scratched tray
to watch those amateurs in boats absurdly active in the bay.
He drinks the sun. His hands are flecked by the rise and slip
of magisterial tides. His asperity is his harbour.

## In the Rigging

Rigging is musical in the tossed bay
as the wind chimes louder, so many invisible
hands playing scatty, frenzied music.

Here are metallic keys without names
jiggling a boisterous tinniness.
He cannot hear them, but is glad to sit

in the sky's window watching the choppy blend
of white horses on gunmetal. On the sill
there is a blue tray, a punnet of nectarines.

There is juice in his beard but how much of him
is still out there in those oily engine rooms,
clambering on vertical ladders that braced and shook

his knees, shooting pains into ankle bones,
with above it all, the roar, the huge vibration
of the turbines that have left him deaf?

He has taken to painting his mistress, the sea,
while his wife, who learned in his long absences
the joys of self-sufficiency, reads and arranges things.

They speak little, never have, but are content to make
a voyage together that no one can ruffle now.
Their one son, visiting with his fair twin daughters,

notes the calm, the ample poise of this salt-licked
        house.
He listens to its rhythms, watching his father, who,
still almost the stranger, washes his sable brushes

carefully, wiping them on clean dry cloths. The girls
go quiet in his presence, in the drift of the window
        wind.
His studies are pensive acreages of tumultuous water.

# The Window Cleaner

He was all of a piece, a man in monochrome,
faded, like the lettering on his cart,
like his overalls and his ancient ladders,
screwed up and wrung out like his shabby chamois
    leathers.
It was always on Tuesday he came, the day of Irish stew.
It was always at that moment called Elevenses,
that regal moment, when Nain, in her stately pom-pom
    slippers,
joined my mother and me in the kitchen,
for her coffee with skin on it,
for the ritual that made my stomach churn.

Lips pursed in concentration,
duly armed with her leprechaun spoon,
she would delicately remove the offending film, then,
with a practised twist of her mottled wrist
would place it decorously in her saucer.
I wanted to look away but never could,
drawn by that clotted horror.

It was now came the knock at the door, there,
ever punctual, with his buckets, wanting water.
He looked so lost he made me nervous,
so small he seemed my size,
like a something left out in the rain.
Was he a grownup, really?

The haunting came years later.
Sat over coffee with my mother
in the kitchen, mine this time, my children's washing
blowing wild outside on a day of big cloud, thin sun . . .
Was it looking up at the window did it,
some sort of déja vu?
'Poor man,' she whispered. 'Who?'
Seems that he went and drowned himself.
She thought I knew.

## Ultrasound Scan

He's not much more than a boy himself,
this doctor in his young white coat.
She notices his eyelashes are deeply curled,
like a child's. How quickly
he has learned the manners of his trade,
blending patterns of solicitude
within protective distancing.

How many children have you had, he asks
as his eyes watch the monitor
and his hand moves the listening device
on her abdomen.
Lying here, absurd,
she is ashamed
of her fuzzy belly and its stretch marks
as she quietly answers – Two,
sensing unspoken criticism,
that she has let herself go, that her flab is more in
    keeping
with a lifetime's farrowing.

She wants to say
They were big babies,
though why she should defend herself
is not made clear.

The pretty radiographer
fiddles with the gauges on the console,
says something, *sotto voce*, to the doctor
catching his green eyes.

She wants to say
They were good boys,
though she has lost them both,
each in his way.

What exactly was the problem, he asks again

and his politeness numbs her.
Eyes blurring
she bites her lip, unable to reply,
knowing no way to describe,
in terms that could make sense to him,
this harrowing thing,
this life of hers,
this broken-hearted womb.

## Replay

I would have gladly walked another road
with you
to build a smiling house of sticks
on a mountainside with stoic pines
goats on long tethers
among these celandines and furze
and childlike themes.

Woken from a stone pragmatic pose
that's second nature now
saluting with surprise
your coming back
into my blandly neutral afternoon
I break into feeling
panic brightly at the sight of you
and such old half-forgotten tenderness.
How can your hands, your hair
be dear to me
still?

Having to say something
to punctuate my shock
I welcome you prosaically
with a voice grown thunderously pale.

## Roulette

It is a pale impossible remembrance you spring
incongrously on me in this brash place.
The check out – bitfer name – and here we stand
with bulging plastic carriers in our hands,
trapped in the shopping flow. A fractious toddler
grabs for some sweets and gets his cold fist slapped.
These are my children. Yes. We could have bred
but ours was a thin experimental bed. A thought
flirts in my head: who would they be, the progeny
of our novitiate? I'd love to meet for coffee, yes,
sometime, but I've a lot to do, like socks to wash
and then I must consider the effect
of The Black Death on mediaeval Europe.
I want to laugh, I really don't know why.
Mesdames, messieurs, please hurry now and take
your partners in the old genetic dance
just one more time. Your bony face grows aquiline
I see. It's so unfair that men improve with age.

## Heirlooms

In the cupboard under the stairs
it still hangs on its nail,
next to the spike for the paid bills:
your father's jacket splashed with paint,
the sleeves rolled up, waiting
to be worn again. A foolishness
of memories. These are only things.

So many layers live
in the cupboard under the stairs.
This glints like an opening eye.
Chipped blue enamel, a black handle,
a lid that simply fits, your grandfather's
can for his cold tea. He died
before you were born but it's still here.

You used it to go blackberrying, so small
they had to hook the brambles down.
In the cupboard under the stairs
the air is warm and sweet with the winds
on Ffordd Criccin. There are ponies
in the far field. In the blue rich sheen
of the fruit, flies well and blink.

Listen, lambs in their last season
are weaving their green sounds. You squelch
in the mud of the ditch, reach up, higher,
further, in the cupboard under the stairs.
Hazed leaves dip their tinted shapes.
Jam darkens its fizz on the stove.
Scratches shine on your face.

## Discoveries

I found them in the wooden step
of the summer house
where we kept the lawn mower,
the decorator's trestles
and the shears. Remembering
your country word for them –
curly buttons,
I smile as I lightly flick
fast coiling bodies to the grass.

And I'm back,
a child again in a warm closed kitchen
returning from a trip to Chester Zoo,
finding grey maggots oozing in the meat safe,
segmented obscenity, crawling
in and out of Sunday's lamb.

It still gets me, not so much
the woodlice in the rotting frame,
as the ants waging war in the dustbin
the orange millipedes raving in the compost.

I blanch, recoil
then feel again your patient kindness.
You took me to a place where frogs had spawned.
We tiptoed in drenched grass
finding them everywhere,
leaping up on our soaked shoes.

You placed one in my hand
and he was beautiful.
His emerald throat pulsed fear.

# The Collector

I think they're made of Indian silver,
the sphinx censers sitting on wide sills
at each end of the Long Gallery.
I trace the lines in their necks
where the metal darkens
to a dull sheen like brass.
Their history is as silent as their eyes.
A riddle breathes in their braced limbs,
the arch of their strained haunches.

Shipped to this eccentric haven,
packed in deep tea chests, waiting,
while the green rot-dripping emptiness
of the roof hole gapes above
and large white pigeons flop
on their high cloud ledges
clogged with straw and droppings,
they guard tall windows in their final place.

This house broke her. A banker's nightmare
screamed in its symmetries. The work, the dream
clawed money and blood. It took her weeks to scrape
centuries of layered varnish from the staircase,
its raw carved brutal fruit, months to stitch
painstakingly, each pleat in the bed hangings
of green Chinese silk. Now uncomprehending tourists
sit cold over scones in bleach-smelling tearooms.

That Louis Quinze chair, its scrolled legs
shedding gilt and frayed braiding
with a sad tawdry sideshow panache, stands
on the first floor landing where the aviary
swoops with the cries of mynahs. Her toucans
scrape their toy painted bills, clack a dull music
against the bars. They are as inscrutable
as the sphinxes, the icy bell in the restored campanile,
the little wet windy gazebo on the East Lawn.

# Kalends

It was the first season.
Japonica sprang on your wall,
crushed red eggshells flecked
on undressed stone.

Your lane was blurred with primroses.

You were gentled, new,
the soft pulse of breeding lighting you.
We talked in your kitchen,
our laughter rising, girlish and strong
among cans of paint and packing cases.

When your child was born it was high summer.

I came in the second season,
paused for the windburned sycamore,
the stream among ferns.
There were berries and barley.

I held your baby, brightly,
till, pierced with loss
my tears were arrows.
I stood in a wide window
of sapphire and late swallows.

You gave me a blessing.

In your daughter's small tenacious clasp
I felt something glow like a crystal.

It will be winter when I come again.
It will be the third season.
I shall bring the man I love.

We shall stand at your door,
in this our long, our last
intensity of innocence.

## Lure

They brought him
soft moustached and stained
from his timber house in the orchard
the company angel, netted now
concealed in his brimmed veiled hat
a bizarre bride, gloved and elegant
to our almond tree, where the swarm
hung like a full gauzed fruit.

It quivered menace.
Go inside, they said, so I watched
from the window, half numb with magic.
He moved like a soft ghost.
His bees made a deep hum.
I knew his grandchildren, their big eyes
and their quietness; his wife, his daughter
small clenched people, invisibly bound.

Fireside devil, they called him.
How should I know what that meant, but
that here was a man of power and sage lore.
He swayed with his boxes, baskets, nets
the signs of his calling, to our safe green place
tracking his creatures, honey brown
flickering like dust motes in the light
from that full bellied gourd.

On a bough of our almond tree
made hallowed, made regal
bearing always now, this, the elect's sign
the stamp of the bees' choice.
By stealth he sealed them his again,
homed back to his plums, his pears
and his white keps; to his webbed people
that still more subtle capture.

# Ceremonial

The fire is whistling.
The branches shift. You catch a drifting piece
of corrugated cardboard, before it flies
and takes its ruby sequinned border to the trees,
singeing the leaves. You prod with a pitchfork.
A fire needs watching at this time of year
though there was rain last night. You felt
it was appropriate to lock yourself within
a task that needed all your concentration.
A bonfire mood. A kind of ritual.

Something is moving in the bonfire's heart.
The boxes curl, are licked by floods of silk.
The smoke will sting. Your hands will be clenched
with soot. For days before you made your preparations.
The scrub you cleared, damson and buddleia,
the leggy forsythia, grown to a towering pitch
that never flowered. You snapped and you chopped small
the sand toned trunks, the shoots of pithy grey.
Each burns with its different note.
A halo furls. Its edge is melting away.

It was good to work in the garden, tearing down,
hacking and making clear. You were glad to sweat,
to bend, to turn yourself into a smudged automaton.
Like cutting cane. Like clearing a track through a jungle.
Suburban gardens can be just as wild as the human
            heart,
still more, the human mind pitched to its limit.
You watched the bonfire's spirit
waste, consume and crystallize, and then when it was
            done
you raked among charcoal, pleased to find peace
among ash, stillness on blackened ground.

## Victrix

I saw a child at the drinking fountain
cupping his hands in expectation
nothing came
he did not seem perturbed
and took a stick
to poke about a bit
his face was set
his mouth was curling at the corners

a little girl appeared
she had an air about her
the boy stepped back
abashed
and in a moment
the bright jet rose for her
deflecting rainbows

she turned
he stood there
silent
tried again

once more the water soared
as magic as before

he let it shrink and sink
frowned
tugged at his socks
and did not drink

## Manikin

someone has left a manikin
on the charred ledge
it must signify something
its limbs have been bound around
meticulously
with bands of coloured wool
it is surmounted with a magpie's feather

it is a pagan thing

strange to find it here
at Saint Seiriol's well
where water bubbles softly in its square
edged by worn flags
a seat of cracked slate set in stone

the wall is stained with damp
thrown coins squint among pebbles
the water tastes sharp, tastes cold
thinly a robin stakes his claim
on a bare elder

you keep coming back
for something you always find
but cannot name
it lives here somewhere
in the old stones, the ivy
the large leafed cresses

you hold the manikin
you twist it in your hand
some sainted hermit
stands within your light
some woman's tears are binding
the bright ply
on the peeled stick

you do not want to leave
you lift tired hands
in thin sun
setting him reverently back
lifting the latch
on a green shape

# Bryn Mair

This is the gaunt sea house

it makes a statement
desolate, empty
but a full statement

and in its sea bleached garden
you climb through salty growth
ground elder, ivy, residual coppices

with here, higher, above the level of the lesser sea fogs
a jungle of holly, pale stemmed polished spiny
where ponies, shaggy with winter
browse daringly with soft creased mouths
shifting, steaming under their smudged green
        blankets
waiting for hay, for sight of the van from the farm
the boys, the bundles, the dusk sharp voices
the gleam of their eyes, their rapt faces

leave the sea garden
its dense sodden grasses
its sad smell that clings to your clothes

take the unmade road that leads to the first of the
        quarries
fenced off now, barricaded, a dark hole, delved,
        depleted
facing, like some mysterious caveat
the Franciscan friary in its grove of larches
where snowdrops spread silver green filigree
seen through railings and rusted gates

here the culverts converge
bubbling under the slab
merging in bright skeins

Our Lady, Star of the Sea
is set back, protected
fringed by soft mosses

swayed by her own baroque extravagance
fluttering the paradox of her marble draperies
her serenity is fixed, is obvious
so, in her artifice she appears uneasy
holding her cold poised child above the world

she is not at home

unlike the snow dredged on the high scarps
unlike the mistletoe glinting on crabbed trees
unlike the bowls in deep windows
starred with wax frail flowers

## Triskel

And if we are the disinherited
assembling here the coiled myth
of our life, in a region budding
at the nodal point
of history's dichotomies

and if we are the treacherous borderers
who, like so many borderers, take care
to listen, all attentiveness
but keep our own allegiance secret,
stoppered tight

you'll find we speak a brightly hybrid tongue
and watch with skill the blowing ways of winds.

We sing the songs of these same simple fisheries
the layered walls here, wall on wall,
whitewashed or flaking umber under eaves,
the smoking range, the griddle oiled and sheened.

And see how the cats of the border barns
are gathering. We'll emulate their self-sufficiency.
Hardy and small these creatures, quite complete,
lop-eared perhaps but richly tortoiseshell.

These are the lords of rafters
and of bales, and would they ever bite
the hand that feeds, these princes
of chipped willow pattern plates
you set on doorsteps of your green dark world?

## Shaman

To find a speech, a tongue
to fit interstices
of this land worn close as a skin.

To climb among blackthorn, cold
cupping of bud white
on black twigs; a scent

is there, thin and shining
as cowslips in floodweather, under
skies of dark geese, deep eddies

of cloud. Here, the high bank
crumbles; fragile roots are prinked
with gobbets of red earth.

What is the sound this land makes
at the far reach of March,
with the lengthening sun, a cleanness

of fresh sap? The speech
of the shaman is locked in the water web
where rivers meet; slowdeep

valley wanderer of the wide meander,
still chuckling mountain freshet,
spate river, riding on pebbles,

not mud, blending watery selves,
distinct as people, below Rhydyddauddwr.
Incompatible are they; slow sluggish

dark flow, quick moody swift
young sprinter to the sea? It was
like this a millenium earlier

at the crossing place. Hear heavy wains,
the whinny of horses, the voices in the dusk;
chill calls, that Norman French nasality,

Tegeingl mingling Mercian – vowels broadening,
lengthening, but never merging with the plaited water
nor interweaving on a loom of water.

The threads remain; sharp, several, sure.

## The Wisdom of the Place

I knew she was there
I knew she would come
she was the wisdom of the place
she belonged here

she was part of the old sorrow
having no sharp corners now
worn down
to this tangible mossed sadness

but how would she appear
and would I fear her
the hag of the high tor
it was not her season yet
but the wind was turning

brittle and bleached
were the speaking grasses
telling something under their breath
that was heresy
that was nameless danger

I would belong here
after this night was over
I would be reborn through fire
I would be reborn through ritual

I would enter the root of the rowan
I would sleep under the sickle
I would climb to the rocking stone
I would know the safety of the salamander
I would know the darkness of the doe
I would learn from the paws of the she-badger
the power under the rock

I would curl in the cup of the acorn
I would fly in the eye of the peregrine
to the soused earth smell of lath and plaster
in the old house on the apple island

I would greet the raven
I would feed her on my wrist
I would wear gold at my neck
my feet bleeding

brown stream that runs through peat
is she waiting under the pines?

quiet pool of the white pebbles
is she sat by the hornbeam?

gentle hare in your form
is she fixed in your fur?

is she hid in the cleft?
is she spread in the rye?
is she found in the field of the red clover?

coldness came over the hill like an army marching
coldness came whistling, lamenting the summer gone

I thought on the zenith
her youthful form in the high meadow
the maiden with her fruits
with her garland of corn

I sit huddled
against the wall of the broken sheepfold
I sit huddled thinking of them
the four men I loved who shared the same face

I think of my sons I cannot understand

to the jubilee tower
and the moon in her full
blowing an ice wind